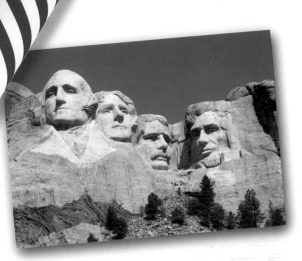

REGIONS OF THE U.S.A.

The Midwest

by Rebecca Felix

PUBLISHED BY THE CHILD'S WORLD ®

Published by The Child's World®
1980 Lookout Drive • Mankato, MN 56003-1705
800-599-READ • www.childsworld.com

Acknowledgments
The Child's World®: Mary Berendes, Publishing Director
Red Line Editorial: Editorial direction
The Design Lab: Design
Amnet: Production
Design Elements: Dreamstime

Photographs ©: Photodisc, title, 3, 4, 7, 10, 11, 13, 21, 23, 28; Jason
Lugo/iStockphoto, 3; Shutterstock Images, title, 29; Red Line Editorial,
Inc., 5, 6; iStockphoto/Thinkstock, 10, 16, 22, 25, 26; North Wind/
North Wind Picture Archives, 15, 17, 31; Hemera/Thinkstock, 19;
Photodisc/Thinkstock, 22; Brand X Pictures, 27

Front cover: Photodisc; Jason Lugo/iStockphoto; MidwestWilderness/
iStockphoto; Shutterstock Images

ISBN: 978-1623234911
LCCN: 2013931425

Printed in the United States of America
Mankato, MN
July, 2013
PA02170

ABOUT THE AUTHOR

Rebecca Felix is a writer and editor who grew up in the Midwest. She received a bachelor's degree in English from the University of Minnesota, which is her home state. She has edited and written several children's books and currently lives in Florida, which is in the Southeastern region of the United States.

Table of Contents

CHAPTER ONE

Plains, Bison, and Blizzards

Rolling, grassy plains and fields of crops stretch for miles. Thousands of lakes dot the landscape. Deer and wolves live in forests. Rivers rush past busy cities. This region of the United States is called the Midwest. It is also known as America's Heartland because of its central geographic location in North America. The Midwest is a national center of population and **industry**. Twelve states make up the Midwest. Iowa, Kansas, Missouri, Nebraska,

Many of the states in the Midwest have miles and miles of farmland.

North Dakota, and South Dakota make up the western part. These are the Great Plains states. The Rocky Mountains border this area to the west. Illinois, Indiana, Michigan, Minnesota, Ohio, and Wisconsin are the Great Lakes states. Each borders at least one of the Great Lakes. The Appalachian Mountains partly border this area to the southeast.

The Midwest is home to many important waterways. In addition to the Great Lakes, the Mississippi River begins its

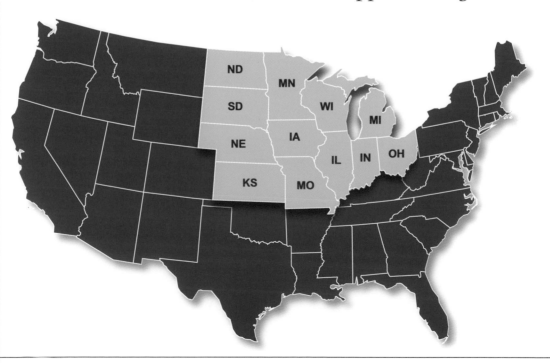

Twelve states make up the Midwest.

2,350-mile (3,782 km) route toward the Gulf of Mexico in northern Minnesota. The Missouri River also cuts through the western part of the region. It meets the Mississippi in Saint Louis, Missouri.

Geography

Glaciers covered the Midwest thousands of years ago. These glaciers moved south, grinding rocks and other materials.

The Great Lakes make up the largest system of freshwater on the surface of the planet.

The Black Hills in South Dakota were formed thousands of years ago.

This movement left behind a rich soil. The glaciers also shaped the landscape. The Midwest is mostly open and flat. But there are rolling hillsides and lakes, too. This area is known as the Central Lowland.

The Central Lowland has many forests. Trees found here include pines, oaks, birch, and maples. West of the Central Lowland are the Great Plains. This land is mostly grassy plains with few trees. The Midwest also includes caves, waterfalls, and rocky lakeshore. Other landforms include plateaus, such as the Ozark Plateau in Missouri. Rock formations such as the Badlands in the Black Hills of South Dakota are also in the Midwest.

Climate

The Midwest experiences big climate changes because the region is not close to oceans. Oceans help **regulate** temperatures. Summers can be very hot and humid in the Midwest. High heat can make **droughts** worse. This combination can lead to wildfires and crop damage. The Midwest can receive a lot of rain in summer, too. The rain can lead to the opposite extreme: floods.

Snow covers much of the Midwest for most of winter. Heavy blizzards are common. Ice forms on cars, roads, and roofs. Temperatures can drop below 0 degrees Fahrenheit (-18°C).

During a heat wave in the summer of 2012, two cities in Kansas reached 115 degrees Fahrenheit (46°C).

Spring and autumn are usually less extreme. Snow melts and **vegetation** comes back to life in the spring. This vegetation includes crops, grass, and leaves from **deciduous** trees that had turned color and dropped in fall.

During summer transitions—spring turning to summer and summer to fall—tornadoes are a threat. The southern part of the Midwest gets hit so often it is known as Tornado Alley.

Wildlife

Many American bison herds lived on the Great Plains a long time ago. They were hunted and almost became extinct. Today, some small herds still live in parts of the Midwest, including in Kansas and South Dakota. White-tailed deer, gray wolves, black bears, and fox live throughout the Midwest. Moose can be found in parts of northern Minnesota. The skies and water are home to many birds, including Canada geese, eagles, and many species of waterfowl. Waterfowl are birds like ducks or loons. Rivers and lakes are full of many types of turtles, frogs, and fish.

Waterfowl are commonly seen in parts of the Midwest.

MIDWEST CAPITALS

Minnesota's capital of Saint Paul faces Minneapolis across the Mississippi River. Together they are called the Twin Cities. In Wisconsin, five lakes surround the capital of Madison. Ann Arbor, Michigan, is home to five universities. Columbus, Ohio, is the capital and Ohio's largest city. Indianapolis, Indiana, hosts several national car races, including the Indy500. Springfield, Illinois, is the third capital city in its state's history. Des Moines, Iowa, was named for the Des Moines River. Jefferson City, Missouri, is named after the third U.S. president, Thomas Jefferson. Lincoln, Nebraska, was originally named Lancaster. Topeka, Kansas, is home to the Hallmark Card plant. Pierre, South Dakota, has the second-smallest population of any state capital in the country. Bismarck, North Dakota, was historically a rowdy town with saloons and shootouts!

CHAPTER TWO

Native Americans, Pioneers, and Industrialists

Paleo-Indians first came to North America thousands of years ago. They were the ancient ancestors of Native Americans. Native Americans spread across the continent and formed tribes. Each tribe spoke a different language and had different customs. Many western Great Plains tribes depended on bison to survive. These tribes included the Dakota (or Sioux), Pawnee, Cheyenne, and Arapaho. Tribes that lived in the eastern Great Plains and near the Great Lakes used hunting and farming to survive. They included

The Louisiana Purchase in 1803 doubled the size of the United States.

the Hopewell, Menominee, Chippewa, Ojibwa, and Potawatomi. Many Native American tribes still exist in the Midwest today, but in fewer numbers. Displacement and decline in population began when Europeans settled in the area.

Creation of Colonies

It is estimated Europeans came to what is now the United States as early as 985. But colonies were not created until the late 1500s and early 1600s. People **immigrated** from Europe throughout the 1600s. They created colonies along the East Coast.

European colonists exposed Native Americans to new diseases they could not cure. This caused many Native

American deaths. European pioneers traveled across the Great Plains claiming land. They wanted to settle this land for farming and living. Native Americans were pushed from areas where they had lived for many years. This created tension and conflict between some colonists and Native Americans.

Wars

Conflicts over land between British and French colonists arose, too. The land that is now Ohio was one area fought over. This fighting led to the French and Indian War from 1754 to 1763. Native American tribes fought for both sides during the war. The war ended with the British taking land from the French. East of the Mississippi River and north to Canada became British land.

The American Revolution began in 1775. American colonists fought for independence from Great Britain. The war lasted until 1783. The British gave control of the Northwest Territory to the United States. This was land

Ohio was the first territory in the Midwest officially to become a state. It has been a state since 1803.

between the Appalachians and Mississippi River that went north to Canada.

The European Industrial Revolution spread to the United States at this time. Throughout the mid-1800s, populations and cities grew. Great growth and change also happened in the agriculture, mining, manufacturing, and transportation industries.

In 1803, the United States purchased a large piece of land controlled by France. This was called the Louisiana Purchase. The United States gained land west of the Mississippi River to the Rocky Mountains. Several of the states in the Midwest were later formed from this land.

The Midwest continues to be a center of industry in the country.

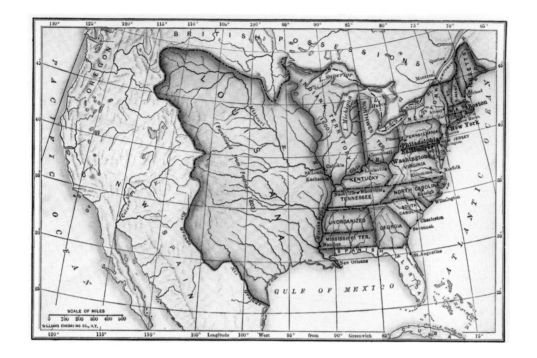

The Louisiana Purchase included land that would later become several states in the Midwest.

Between 1854 and 1859 was a violent time in the Kansas territory. Conflict over slavery led to many deaths. This time is known as Bleeding Kansas. Some believe these events helped lead to the U.S. Civil War. The U.S. Civil War started in 1861 and lasted four years. The conflict was between Northern and Southern states. The Northern states, which included the Midwest, wanted to end slavery. The South did not. Slavery was ended when the war was over.

EXPLORING THE MIDWEST

Following the Louisiana Purchase, explorers Meriwether Lewis and William Clark traveled the new U.S. territory. They set off from Saint Louis in 1804. They crossed Missouri and Kansas. They traveled along the border of Nebraska and Iowa. Then they crossed South Dakota and moved into North Dakota. The explorers stayed in Fort Mandan, North Dakota, for the winter. Then they headed west toward the Pacific Ocean. Lewis and Clark recorded what they saw during their travels. They saw prairie dogs, bison, deer, and bears. They made new plant discoveries. They also revealed useful information on the area's rivers and landscape.

Present Day

Industrialization continued in the Midwest throughout the 1800s and 1900s. The Midwest is still a busy industrial center of the nation. The Midwest's agricultural history and small population of native tribes also remain.

CHAPTER THREE

Community, Corn, and Cars

Each state's government has three branches. The head of each state's executive branch is the governor. The governor is elected to ensure state laws are carried out. The governor also oversees state programs and policies.

Another branch is the legislative branch. Members of the state legislature write what will become laws. They also handle the state's budget and taxes. To do these jobs, most states have two chambers, or groups. This keeps power balanced. Nebraska is the only U.S. state that has only one legislative chamber.

In all states in the Midwest except Kansas, governors must be a minimum age to hold office.

The Illinois State Capitol building houses all three branches of the state's government.

A state's judicial branch is responsible for its court systems. State courts take care of non-criminal cases such as someone not paying taxes. Courts also hear cases when a person breaks a state law.

State governments oversee the local governments of counties and cities, too. Local governments manage housing, parks, and police and fire departments.

The Midwest has been the center of important national political movements. The Progressive Movement started in the early 1900s in Wisconsin. The movement centered on making the nation more modern and industrialized. It became a political party called the Progressive Party. A Wisconsin senator ran for president in 1924 under this party.

Every four years, some U.S. states hold caucuses. A caucus is a gathering where U.S. presidential candidates are discussed. There is a vote on who should move forward in the process. Iowa's caucus is considered very important because it is first. Many media members and politicians travel to Iowa during the caucus. The event has national importance.

Economy

Agriculture has been important in the Midwest's **economy** throughout history. The quality of soil and the landscape create an excellent environment. It is good for growing crops and raising hogs and cattle. Farms in the Midwest produce a

Wisconsin was home to more than 1 million dairy cows in 2011!

lot of the country's food, especially grain products. Because of this, the region is often called America's Breadbasket. Grain products are used to make cereal, pastas, bread, animal feed, and more. They are a major **export** of the Midwest. Iowa is the top producer of corn in the entire country. Kansas is the top wheat producer.

Wisconsin is a top dairy producer. It is sometimes called America's Dairyland. It produces more cheese than any other state. Wisconsin is also one of the top producers of milk.

One of the Midwest's top exports is dairy from Wisconsin.

Many states in the Midwest are located in the center of the country. This makes them important for transporting goods. Along the Mississippi River there are lumber mills, grain mills, and sawmills. Manufacturing iron and steel is big near the Great Lakes. Indiana is also a top manufacturer of iron, steel, and oil products. North Dakota has become a national leader in oil. An oil rush in recent years created a booming economy there.

The oil rush has created a growing economy in North Dakota.

TOURISM

There are many sights to see in the Midwest. The Mall of America is in Bloomington, Minnesota. It has more than 500 stores. The Gateway Arch is a famous landmark in Saint Louis, Missouri. Branson, Missouri, is a center of entertainment that has many shows, museums, and amusement parks. Wisconsin Dells is called the waterpark capital of the world. Chicago is the third-biggest U.S. city by population. It is home to deep-dish pizza and a lively jazz music scene. The Black Hills in South Dakota have many sights to see, such as Mount Rushmore and the Badlands.

Automobiles are another major export in the Midwest. Three of the top U.S. automakers are based in Michigan. Known as the "Big Three," these include Ford, General Motors, and Chrysler.

CHAPTER FOUR

Hot Dish and Mild Manners

People have many ideas about cultures and people in the Midwest. Some ideas are partly true but others are incorrect. Many believe cultures and **ethnicities** across the Midwest are the same. A lot of Midwesterners come from European backgrounds, especially Scandinavian countries. But not every Midwesterner does. People from all over the world live across the Midwest today.

A person's background and ethnicity can influence his or her way of life. So can the person's surroundings. People living in rural areas may have different ways of life than those in urban areas. The Great Plains area is more rural than the

Minnesota is known as the Land of 10,000 Lakes. But there are actually approximately 12,000 lakes that people swim, fish, and enjoy.

Great Lakes area. There are urban cities throughout the Midwest. These include Minneapolis, Chicago, Saint Louis, Detroit, Indianapolis, and Milwaukee. As of 2011, more than 67 million people lived in the Midwest.

Agriculture is important in many rural areas. Other Midwesterners live in urban areas where the arts and industry are celebrated. Across the Midwest, people hold county and state fairs to celebrate all these things together. Midwesterners also enjoy many different outdoor activities.

State fairs in the Midwest are known for their foods. And many of the foods are served on a stick!

Chicago, Illinois, is the biggest city in the Midwest.

People swim, canoe, and fish the rivers and lakes. In the winter, people ice fish on frozen lakes. Hunting is another popular activity. People hunt deer, ducks, pheasant, turkeys, and bighorn sheep.

Midwesterners are usually thought to be hard-working and friendly people. People believe Midwesterners are practical and do not take risks. This may be common, but it is not true of all people living across the 12 states.

Food

Food in the Midwest is considered simple, without much spice. Dishes are often made with goods produced in the region. This means a lot of breads, corn, pork, poultry, and beef. Walleye, trout, bison, and wild rice are also a few local foods. Ethnic backgrounds have an influence. Scandinavian dishes are common.

Michigan and Minnesota are among the only states in which people say *pop* instead of *soda*.

The Midwest is called America's Breadbasket because it grows all the crops needed to make bread.

RECIPE

MICROWAVE WILD RICE HOT DISH

Ingredients:

1 cup uncooked wild rice

2 cups chicken broth

1 teaspoon salt

9 tablespoons butter

8 ounces canned mushrooms, sliced

1 ounce minced onions

Directions:

Wash and soak wild rice for 2 hours in tap water. Pour chicken broth, salt, and 1 tablespoon of butter into a 3-quart covered casserole dish. Cook in the microwave on high for 6–7 minutes. Add wild rice and cook on defrost for 50 minutes. In a separate microwave-safe container, melt 8 tablespoons of butter. Add mushrooms and onions to this container. Cook on high for 2–3 minutes. Stir ingredients each minute. Next, add these ingredients to the rice and cook on defrost for 10–15 minutes. Let stand in the microwave for 5 minutes after cooking.

Fast Facts

Population: 67,316,297 (2012 estimate)

    Most populous state: Illinois (12,875,255, 2012 estimate)

    Least populous state: North Dakota (699,628, 2012 estimate)

Area: 822,718 square miles (2,130,830 sq km)

Highest temperature: 121 degrees Fahrenheit (49°C), tied by Kansas and North Dakota in 1936

Lowest temperature: minus-60 degrees Fahrenheit (-51°C), tied by Minnesota in 1996 and North Dakota in 1936

Largest cities: Chicago, Illinois; Indianapolis, Indiana; Columbus, Ohio; Detroit, Michigan; Milwaukee, Wisconsin

Major sports teams: Chicago Bulls (NBA, basketball); Cincinnati Reds (MLB, baseball); Detroit Red Wings (NHL, hockey); Green Bay Packers, (NFL, football); Indianapolis Colts (NFL, football); Kansas City Chiefs (NFL, football); Minnesota Twins (MLB, baseball)

Glossary

deciduous (di-SIJ-oo-uhs) Deciduous trees lose their leaves in fall. Most deciduous leaves turn colors such as yellow, orange, or red in the fall.

droughts (drouts) Droughts are long periods of time without rain. Droughts can lead to crops drying up.

economy (i-KON-uh-mee) Economy is the system of making, buying, and selling things. Agriculture is large part of the economy in the Midwest.

ethnicities (eth-NIH-sit-ees) Ethnicities are associations with certain groups of people of the same culture. There are people of many ethnicities in the Midwest.

export (EK-sport) An export is a product made in one place and sold to another place. Grains are a major export of the Midwest.

immigrate (IM-i-grate) People immigrate from another country. Many European people immigrated to the United States.

industry (IN-duh-stree) An industry is a group of businesses. The lumber industry is important to the Midwestern economy.

regulate (REG-yuh-late) To regulate is to manage or control. The Midwest is too far from oceans to have them regulate temperature.

vegetation (vej-uh-TAY-shun) Vegetation is the different plants in an area. The Midwest has a variety of vegetation, including many types of grasses.

To Learn More

Books

Johnson, Robin. *What's in the Midwest?* New York: Crabtree, 2011.

Rau, Dana Meachen. *The Midwest*. New York: Scholastic, 2012.

Stone, Tanya Lee. *Regional Wild America: Unique Animals of the Midwest*. Detroit, MI: Blackbirch Press, 2005.

Web Sites

Visit our Web site for links about the Midwest:

childsworld.com/links

Note to Parents, Teachers, and Librarians: We routinely verify our Web links to make sure they are safe and active sites. So encourage your readers to check them out!

Index